Taking Good Care of Your Cat

Table Of Contents

Foreword

Chapter 1:
Cat Care Basics

Chapter 2:
Visiting The Vet

Chapter 3:
What You Need To Know About Vaccinations

Chapter 4:
Provide The Correct Food

Chapter 5:
Provide The Correct Grooming

Chapter 6:
Provide The Correct Toys And Affection

Chapter 7:
The Downfall Of Not training Your Cat

Wrapping Up

Foreword

There are a few areas that need to be covered concerning cat care basics and all these issues are of primary concern when the individual is keen on keeping a pet, especially a cat.

Caring For Your Cat

Chapter 1:
Cat Care Basics

Synopsis

The following are usually some areas of concern when it comes to cat care basics:

Basic Information

If the new owner is not interested in feeding the pet cat processed food products, home made preparations will easily suffice. However, one should always try and avoid giving the cat table scraps as the main food source for the cat, as human food is not really complete and nutritious for the cat. The essential ingredients for cat food should be amino acid taurine and calcium which usually come in the form of a bone based meal.

Another basic cat requirement would be the litter box for its toilet facility. This should ideally be placed in a quiet area, where there is some privacy for the cat and no distractions to startle it when attempting to do its business.

As cats are naturally inclined to scratch various objects, such as furniture and curtains, it would be in the owner's best interest to find ways to keep the pet cat from doing this very damaging act. Some people use sticky tape and tin foil on surfaces that would initially seem temping to the cat to scratch on, while others spray the area with scents, as generally cats dislike strong smells. Purchasing a scratching post is another alternative and the cat should be encouraged to use this instead of the furniture which is more often than not more tempting to the cat.

Providing the cat with an adequate amount of toys to keep it occupied will ensure it does not get into mischief when bored.

Chapter 2:
Visiting The Vet

Synopsis

Most animals have a natural aversion to visiting the vet, as this is usually done under unpleasant circumstances. However, as this is a necessary part of the cat's life, some measures should be taken to make this as easy as possible for both the owner and the cat.

Keeping Them Healthy

First, the main mode of transporting the cat is the pet carrier. Measures should be taken to try and get the cat to refrain from associating this with only visits to the vet. This is because the prospect of visiting the vet is never an enjoyable one in the cat's mind. Therefore, taking the cat out in the pet carrier for less stressful reasons will help to confuse the cat sufficiently, so that it does not associate the carrier with the vet visits.

Cats often find the carrier confining, which leads to their natural dislike and aversion towards it. Adding a favorite toy in with the cat may help to eliminate some of the stress the cat undergoes while being confined to such as small place. Placing a cloth over the carrier when in transit will also help to reassure the cat and calm it down as the darkness will give it some sense of quiet and perhaps even encourage a nap.

Taking the trouble to find a good and caring vet that is inclined to make the animal feel comfortable before actually starting the examination session is also another thing to consider when it comes getting the cat calm and accepting. If the cat is comfortable, then it is less likely to squirm and create a fuss. This will also be less stressful for both the owner and the cat. Some vets keep treats handy to try and get the cat to calm down and be more settled during the visit.

Chapter 3:
What You Need To Know About Vaccinations

Synopsis

Although vaccinations are often a feared necessity, there are still a lot of problems that are usually associated with getting an animal to conform and accept this as important and unavoidable. However, the owner should be steadfast in getting all the required vaccinations for the pet cat as it will help to keep the cat in better health conditions.

Important Facts

Vaccinations are usually administered to provide an animal with the necessary help to keep their body safe from any outside invasion of organisms that will cause the cat to be sick. The cat's immune system should be well guarded against all negative foreign intrusions, hence the necessity of the vaccinations. With the vaccinations, the cat's immune system is able to withstand any onslaught from negative intrusion that may cause the cat's health to deteriorate.

Cat's that are not house bound are usually at higher risk of being exposed to disease causing organisms and thus the consequences of infection are always present. There is also the possibility of such conditions eventually affecting the owner of the cat and those around. One particular alarming disease which the owner can be exposed to is rabies, thus the need for vaccinations.

The following are some of the more popularly recommended vaccines for cats:

• Feline pan leukopenia virus vaccine – this vaccination is meant to keep the cat from contracting a highly infectious disease which can lie dormant before is actually causes fatal reactions.

• Feline claicivirus/herpes virus vaccine – this is meant to treat upper respiratory tract diseases which are prevalent in cats, which most cats are never completely free of but the vaccination helps to keep in under control.

- Rabies virus vaccine – in most countries, it is now mandatory to ensure the cat is inoculated with this as this disease is not only a threat to the cat but also to humans.

Chapter 4:

Provide The Correct Food

Synopsis

Choosing food for the pet cat is not about simply providing it with the types of food it enjoys eating. These types of food are is often not nutritious or well balanced. Therefore, there is a need to ensure all the various elements are present in the cat diet to ensure optimal health conditions for the cat.

Provide Proper Nutrition

There is really no need to know a lot about cat foods and diets, as the owner would only need to know a few facts, mainly based on the cat's statistics, to make an informed decision on the types of foods required. These facts should include the age of the cat, its size, the lifestyle and history of the cat and its breed type. All these would be a good starting point for the owner to make an informed decision on what types of foods are suitable for their pet cat.

As some cat foods are designed to fit into specific categories such as the age of the cat, its nutritional needs and its probable eating capabilities, the owner will be less challenged in making the most appropriate choice. There is a variety of choices for the cat which include dry and wet foods. Either a combination of the two or just one type would be sufficient for the cat as it usually covers a whole spectrum of vitamins and minerals that the cat would need for optimal health.

As budget is probably the main dictating factor when it comes to purchasing the most appropriate foods for the cat, most brands will suffice. However, if cost is not an issue, then making the effort to purchase premium or natural cat food products would be the ideal option, as the quality of such products would be far better than the regular ones on the shelf.

Chapter 5:
Provide The Correct Grooming

Synopsis

Cat are naturally quite fastidious, thus there is a need to be constantly grooming them. Most cats will spend quite some time licking themselves clean and keeping every fur in place.

Keep Them Clean

Long haired cats can be particularly hard to up keep and the owner will have to be committed to constantly grooming the cat. Even the cat itself will spend the better half of a day licking every hair into place. This of course is not really good as the cat is likely to eventually suffer from hairballs and get its coat all matted up. The owner would ideally have to engage the services of a pet groomer to keep the coat manageable and also brush the cat regularly to remove any clumps of hair or excessive hair. Short hair cats are no different as they too need grooming attention and this would include the owner setting aside time daily to brush their coats.

This hair bushing routine is very important and can sometimes be the difference between the cat enjoying a good quality of life and having to run to the vet for an emergency operation to remove a hairball clogging its intestinal track. Daily brushing will help to minimize the amount of hair the cat swallows through its own grooming sessions. Cats often protect themselves by coughing up these hairballs and this can be quite nasty to handle but a better alternative than having a surgical procedure done.

Having some of the tools handy at home would help to create a daily routine that would be enjoyable for both the cat and the owner. Initially the cat may not be too excited about being brushed, but if the owner is persistent and gentle, the cat will eventually come around and learn to accept it as part of the daily necessary routine.

Chapter 6:

Provide The Correct Toys And Affection

Synopsis

Cats love to give and receive attention, but usually on their own terms. This is often hard to understand, especially is the owner is the type that loves to cuddle up with his or her pets. However, there are ways to extended love to a cat without being rebuffed.

The Right Gifts

The following are some tips of how to be affectionate toward a pet cat and the correct toys needed to make the equation complete:

• Although cats are not enormously fond to cuddling up, there are instances when they will allow themselves to be picked up for a quick and gentle cuddle. However, once the cat becomes fidgety, it's time to ease up.

• Cats love to play and the most suitable toys need not be the expensively designed ones. Simple toys made of scraps of paper rolled into a ball or simply scrunched up make perfect toys for the cat. However, the size should be too big to swallow. Dangling a string or dangling something on a string will be a very attractive prospect for the cat's immediate attention. Running it along the floor will really excited the cat and usually ensue a healthy and happy workout for the cat.

• Cats also enjoy being stroked, petted or scratched, however they are rather picky on the areas they allow anyone to come in contact with. Initially, the owner would have to put up with a few scratches before finding the ideal areas the cat would like the attention focused on. The popular spots include under the chin and around the cheeks and also behind the ears and sometimes across the back just before it meets the tail.

- Colorful small balls with bells inside are another popular toy that most cats enjoy playing with. However, the balls should be just big enough so that the cat cannot swallow it.

Chapter 7:
The Downfall Of Not training Your Cat

Synopsis

Untrained cats can prove to be quite a menace to the owner and those around. The belongings of the owner are not to be spared either, as the untrained cat knows no bounds and will react as it see and feels fit.

Why Training Is So Important

There are several elements to contend with when the owner has failed to consider training the pet cat early on. Some of these would include having to deal with toilet training problems, furniture being destroyed indiscriminately, items going missing and a whole host of other things.

When it comes to addressing the toilet training, the cat that is not trained will think nothing of simply using any place suitable to its thought process for this purpose. Therefore, the owner is likely to be cleaning up after the cat and not to mention the awful stink that this will create in the immediate environment. It should be noted that cat's urine and feces have extremely strong odors.

Another problem would be the scratching habits of the cat which would be unleashed on almost anything and everything. However, the primary object that would suffer the most would be the sofa and the carpets. Cats seem to enjoy digging their nails into these items as it seems to provide some primal pleasurable relief for the cat. Having to replace furniture periodically is not a workable option and some form of curbing tactics should be enforced.

Cat's stealing things is also another very popular complaint from owners who don't seem to see the merits of training their cats. Cats are curios by nature and love to explore, thus finding objects that are fascinating to them would result in them trying to keep it for themselves, thus the hiding instinct.

Wrapping Up

Keeping your feline in line can sometimes be quite a tricky task to accomplish. It is possible, it just takes some hard work and effort from both the pet and the owner. As mentioned before, there are many tools that can be used in the training process of the cat to make the process much simpler. With proper use of tools and the tips you have just learned about, you and your cat should be able to share your home with minimal issues. Good luck!

www.ingramcontent.com/pod-product-compliance
Lightning Source LLC
LaVergne TN
LVHW020509080526
838202LV00057B/6263